William Adolphus Clark

Our Modern Athens

Poem

William Adolphus Clark

Our Modern Athens
Poem

ISBN/EAN: 9783744653053

Printed in Europe, USA, Canada, Australia, Japan

Cover: Foto ©Thomas Meinert / pixelio.de

More available books at **www.hansebooks.com**

OUR
MODERN ATHENS;

OR,

WHO IS FIRST?

𝔄 𝔓𝔬𝔢𝔪.

BY

ANICETUS,

AUTHOR OF "HARRY LEROY, OR THE FATALITY OF CRIME;" "HUMAN NATURE, OR THE HEART UNVEILED;" "THE WALK;" "GENIUS, ITS FATE," ETC.

BOSTON:
FOR SALE BY REDDING & CO.,
No. 8 STATE STREET.
1860.

Entered according to Act of Congress, in the year 1860, by

W. A. CLARK,

In the Clerk's Office of the District Court of the District of Massachusetts.

DEDICATION.

To all those who love the truth better than the mere conventionalities of life, through which is perpetrated so much of crying and inhuman wrong, — so much of shameful imposture! — who honor that courage which, fearless of consequences, dares to denounce the votaries of evil and of folly, — who love truth for its sake, and prefer an honest censure to a cowardly, sycophantic acquiescence, silence, and obsequiousness, — who feel that there is a God, and a judgment at his hands, when these bodies which we now inhabit are resolved into their primitive dust, — who delight in satire, when it aims to improve those it assails, — who believe that it is possible to laugh persons out of snobbery and toadyism, when they cannot be kicked or driven, — who think that there is some truth in the declaration that man was made in the image of his Maker, to work out, by his talents, some good for himself and others, — who reverence the *divine* will, and hail with irrepressible delight the outworking of it in mankind, — who live not in the mere exteriors of the mind, but dwell mostly in those beautiful vales of the soul from whence is seen the gorgeous lights of *Heaven*, and where is heard the melodious whisperings of Jehovah and the angels, — who fear not to applaud and defend whenever they are pleased, — who are of honorable conscience, — who believe in the resurrection of the dead, and the life to come, — who despise all meanness, and love a brave, earnest, and daring spirit, — who tremble not when *fools* command, — in fine, who are *men* and *women;* not caricatures of mankind; — to these, and such as these, we dedicate our humble verse; knowing that they, at least, will appreciate our motives, and commend our labor.

ANICETUS.

M189007

PREFACE.

There are, in "Modern Athens," very many individuals who are not only uncertain as to their position, but are quite doubtful as to who are and who are not first. This is a problem which Euclid could easily have solved, and which the author of this verse has met with no difficulty in unravelling. He trusts that the fact of its being in the dress of doggerel, will not make it any the less acceptable to those who can derive a pleasure even in the study of *stones;* — and many such there are. We geologize a somewhat *softer* matter, and by availing, in a measure, of the science of chemistry, we render our labors doubly interesting, to those who may feel any interest whatever. It is to these that we appeal for support, in our effort to laugh at the insolence, the vulgarity, and foppery of a large number in our "Modern Athens," who, assuming to be first, use their best wit to make themselves ridiculous in the extreme.

We have been pointed in our allusion to some persons, who are especially open to the attacks of satirists; and though we disclaim all personal hostility to them, we confess a deep-seated repugnance to their manners and ideas. It is our privilege, as it is the privilege of all men, to amuse ourselves and others at the expense of those who offend by the exhibition of certain habits of life which are at variance with good taste, and a libel on humanity. We do not suppose we shall escape the animadversions of the individuals whom we have hit; and it is possible we may be hit in return. We do not apprehend, however, any very serious bruises; none, at least, that we shall not, in our good physical condition, be able to survive. We have thought there are a large number of sensible people in this community, who would welcome any attempt to put down the insolence of that monied aristocracy, which is so insufferable, and so vulgar, eminating as it does from narrow minds, infected with the coarsest ambition and weakest moral tone. We claim no especial merit for the verse, aside from its purpose; and we sincerely trust that no critic will be stupid enough to criticize us as a *poet*, as was the case when we put forth our former production, "The Walk." Upon that occasion an astute somebody, who was attached to the *Saturday Evening Express*, availed himself of his position to laugh at our *poetry*, when any one but a chucklehead — a full-blooded bumpkin — would have seen with half an eye the verse was intended as doggerel, and pretended to nothing more. But unfortunately for authors, as we have hinted in our present production, the press is sadly deficient in good literary critical talent. Men who write up the news of the day set themselves up as censors and judges of authorship, when, in point of fact, they are, in many cases, totally ignorant of the subject they make bold to handle. We have only to say, so far as we are concerned it is a matter of no moment whether they are quacks or not; but there are those who seek through their genius the public favor, and endeavor to earn a livelihood by their pen. Such ought to be spared the stupidity of critics who cannot write their vernacular correctly, and do not know a "hawk from a hernshaw."

With these remarks, by way of preface, we respectfully invite the reader to the banquet of amusement which is embodied in "Our Modern Athens; or, Who is First?" If encouraged in this little affair, we shall continue our efforts to *assist* in beating down those notions, peculiar to a certain class in this community, which, while innocent enough in themselves, operate deleteriously on persons at large.

We have in MS. a novel, with the same title as this verse, (although entirely independent of it), which would make up into a book of about 600 pp. 12mo. It covers the whole ground of snobbery, and displays in full the ideas of all classes of citizens. We have offered it to the publishers, and although they think it "an original and capital thing," it is our misfortune to be a new author; and their policy is not to *make* authors, but to be made by them. Truly a cute notion.

We subjoin a synopsis of our novel, and should be happy of any offers of publication from those who are desirous of seeing the sham aristocracy of Boston cuffed most soundly, in a work full of incident and dramatic effect.

OUR MODERN ATHENS; Or, Who is First?
A Novel. By ANICETUS.

This novel opens with a disquisition on wealth, embodying the Socratic idea. Then follows a scene with a beggar, in which he is kicked from the door-steps of the dwelling of a snob, — a wealthy aristocrat residing on one of the most fashionable streets. A little boy, by the name of Willie Andrews, observing the act, stops and commiserates him; he is soon joined by a little girl, named Nelly Penniman, a playmate. The father of the girl passes, who is another purse-proud snob, and in an angry manner sends the girl home, commanding her never again to be seen in the company of beggars and low boys — musician's sons! Willie Andrews goes home with the beggar, determined to be his friend. The beggar dies from the effect of his ill treatment, on the bosom of Andrews, to whom he bequeaths a pet dog, called "Bone." Nelly Penniman, whom Willie loved, had been prevented all association with the boy. She forms an intimacy with a college student, by name McAlpin, the son of a man of wealth and genius. This alliance is presented so as to define clearly the manner in which mere snobbery works itself in with true refinement and culture. The marriage is fully sketched, and the sharpest ridicule is fired at the ceremony, which took place in church, whence all were excluded not expressly invited. Willie's disgust at the pride of the Pennimans; his sorrow at Nelly's desertion of him; his vow of revenge; his father's noble charge to let his *virtues* be his revenge. Ida Robinson; her intimacy with Willie stated. The mysterious box taken from the beggar's room; its record of the beggar. Willie fears his love for Ida is not a true passion; her misery. Boston Common sketched, and some noted citizens portratured; passing of the snobs in their carriages through the adjacent streets. Willie and Ida's walk; their comments on the families whose dwellings they pass. The Pennimans soundly laughed at, with their large and costly library *unread;* the ball they give in honor of their daughter's wedding sketched and satirized. Willie's clerkship to the Catchpennies, who are persons aiming to get into the Penniman set. The Catchpennies' tea-table; meeting there of snobs, among whom are Mrs. Touchmenot and her daughter Clasp-me-tighter; Willie's bold talk, and the Touchmenots' indignation; Mrs. Catchpenny's discomforture; her daughter's *nonchalance;* Wille's retreat from the house; an amusing conversation between Mrs. Catchpenny and her daughter, on "sets." Willie in the Public Garden, on the evening of his retreat from the Catchpennies' tea-table; his merriment while seated on one of the benches, over Mrs. Touchmenot's rage. The strange woman; her meeting with Willie; their recognition; Willie's happiness to have met once again the girl who sang so sweetly and was so beautiful, whom he had seen for the first time when he accompanied the beggar home, in a small house directly opposite the beggar's home; their walk. The man in a black cloak; his mysterious appearance; Willie's apprehensions; the woman's caution; Willie's encounter with the ruffian; the oath; the woman's (Agnes Farrady's) account of this man — a broken-down aristocrat, who wanted her for a *mistress.*

Willie's discharge from the Catchpennies'; his enemies;
his courage and self-reliance; his mother's tears; an
affecting interview. Agnes Farrady denounced; Willie's
defence; the meeting of Agnes, Willie, and his mother
and father; their acceptance of Agnes; her excentric
course of life satisfactorily explained. Old Mr. Andrews'
death; his explanation of the process of death, while under-
going dissolution. Agnes' success in reforming harlots;
their gratitude. Prostitution pictured, and the means
suggested to circumscribe it, and root it out. The sons-
in-law of the Pennimans shown in their dissipated habits.
Agnes and Willie; her history continued; their sweet
love. The Atlays! a family of true dignity; their con-
trast with snobs. Lucy Atlay's interest in Willie An-
drews stated. Art discussed. Augustus Hamilton the
friend of Willie; his love of Lucy considered. Mrs.
Robert McAlpin (formerly Miss Nelly Penniman) writes
from Italy; her letters, in which Mrs. McAlpin states her
dear Robert will drink, and is so self-willed there is no
doing anything with him. Agnes Farrady; her encounter
with the ruffian who conceals himself in her house; his
death. Ida Robertson's love for Willie; her jealousy of
Agnes; her interview with Willie; her rage and death.
Willie's home at Lexington described; his genius consid-
ered; his study of the law; Agnes Farrady's love sustains
him; true happiness pictured. Mrs. McAlpin's return
from Europe; her visit to Willie; her offensive manners;
her repulse. Round Hill Water-cure introduced; co-
quetry illustrated. Nahant; snobbery drawn, as observed
at this fashionable watering-place. Mrs. McAlpin's in-
terview here with a southerner; her husband's rage; the
quarrel; the combat; flight of parties from Nahant; the
scandal-mongers at work. Captain Gasious, a half-breed
Cuban, and the Touchmenots. Mrs. Penniman's agita-
tion at the reports about her children; meeting of snobs
at her house to tea; the Catchpennies feel insulted, and
retire in a rage. Willie Andrews' reputation as a lawyer;
his great success; he gains a suit against old Penniman,

who sneered at him when a boy, because a musician's son. A famous drinking saloon; Captain Gasious and fashionable young men drawn; Willie Andrews' meeting, at this place, with Robert McAlpin; his superiority illustrated, and his bold defiance of all pretention unsupported by merit. Willie's meeting with old Penniman; their mutual disgust; the triumph of Willie's eye; the parvenu and snob awed by the power of *merit*. The Pennimans' chagrin at Willie's prosperity; *he* was rapidly rising, while McAlpin was rapidly *falling;* their regrets that Nelly did not marry Andrews. Agnes and Willie; their popularity in society; the praise lavished upon them. Willie, who is now a member of the Suffolk Bar, is regarded as a most promising lawyer; he again wins a suit against Penniman; the old man's rage; his wife's mortification at being obliged to give up her carriage; their fear and hate of Andrews. Old Penniman's depression. Captain Gasious and Mrs. Penniman; their indiscretion; Penniman's discovery; his sudden death. The Catchpennies' failure; their shame. Robert McAlpin's death; his family's joy; Nelly McAlpin's visit to Willie's office; her love for him expressed; his indifference; her madness and death. The Atlays' friendship for Willie rewarded; Lucy is married to his bosom friend, Hamilton. Hamilton and Willie's mutual love contrasted with the heartlessness of snobbery. Mrs. Penniman's death, and the full triumph of Willie over those who had sneered at him when a boy; — fulfilling the charge of his father, to revenge himself for the insult of the Pennimans by his *virtues;* and realizing the words of the old beggar, that in his eye was a genius which in future years would make him famed.

This is but a faint outline of the work, from which may be gathered something of its scope and design. Any one who has $1500 to $2000 to risk in the publication of this novel can have the MS. for examination, by applying to the author, through Redding & Co., 8 State St.

A.

January, 1860.

WEALTH is the smallest thing on earth, — the least gift that God has bestowed on mankind. What is it in comparison with God's word? — what in comparison with corporal gifts, or those of the understanding — wisdom! Yet are men most eager after it when it has neither material, formal, efficient, nor final cause, nor anything else that is good; therefore our Lord God *commonly gives riches to those from whom he withholds spiritual good.*
MARTIN LUTHER'S *"Table Talk."*

This much the poet must necessarily borrow from the philosopher, as to be master of the common topics of morality. He must at least be speciously honest, and in all appearance a friend of virtue throughout his poem. The good and wise will abate him nothing in this kind; and the people, though corrupt, are, in the main, best satisfied with his conduct. SHAFTSBURY.

It is with narrow-souled people as with narrow-necked bottles: the less they have in them, the more noise they make in pouring out.
POPE.

So in the grave shall we as quiet lie,
Miss'd by some few that loved our company;
But some so like to thorns and nettles live,
That when they perish none for them can grieve.
WALLER. — *From the French.*

OUR MODERN ATHENS;

OR,

WHO IS FIRST?

Our Modern Athens! great in little things,—
In notions vast, whence pride exultant springs;
Stuffed with great men whose tough and hard-worked brains,
Ne'er weary thinking with the greatest pains;
Known to the world as the fine city where,
Talent is cherished with the tend'rest care;
Rich in commerce, banks, and the art of trade,
Which cities build where men their gold parade;
We hail thee great in little things and big,
When caution may be used, yet *cutely* hid;
Be ours the task to trace in jingling rhyme,
Thy snobs and worthies of the present time;—
Be ours the task to tell in what thou art
Nonsensical,— in what supremely smart;
To point the eye to those who rate as first,
And wield the power of the kingly purse.

In days of yore, when freedom was a joy,
And in sweet truth our fathers sought employ,—

Living to learn life's solemn duties well,
Unmixed with atheist, Jew, or infidel, —
There was a glory stern in Pilgrim mind,
In vain we look in later days to find.
Not that we would in all the Pilgrim be, —
Assume his virtues and deformity;
No; but from decay we would gladly save,
The manners plain that marked him to the grave; —
The honor true with which he dealt with man,
And lived a Christian in a Christian land.

Unlike to these are they who now possess,
The soil whereon a nation's birthplace rests.
Their god is mammon, — their high hopes are here,
Where beef is fat, and cheap is lager beer;
Where getting dimes at sure and rapid rate,
Is deemed the *freedom* foremost in the State.
Heaven *may* be, yet what more bliss divine,
Can mortals know " than living to their mind,"
Blessed with spring beds, good sleep, and all besides, —
From genteel servants to most genteel wives?
Merry they go, and merry, sometimes fall;
By " rushing business," — 'tempting to be " tall;"
But that's no matter; up they get again,
And " at it go," like fresh and hopeful men.

" Our Modern Athens," killed with pride and fuss,
Is of earth earthy, — must return to dust;
Then why should *she* turn up her attic nose
At other cities, which less of thinking does,
Of getting, keeping, making a fine show, —
Of learning, trading, how things *ought* to go?
Our Boston Yankee, like his city grand,
Is a cute, staid, and, O, most proper man!

If he's to teach he teaches with an air,
That signifies he's *first*, and dares compare;
There's no degree he will accept but first;
And sooner than be second would be hers'd,
For the tomb and lay his insulted head,
Amid the ashes of his kindred dead.
First! ay, there is no proper grade but that,
Which each assume, — from genius to the flat;
But not alone th' author and pedagogue,
Would command from men obedient nod;
This self-esteem and love of fame prevail
In quarters all, — each attic breast assail.
The boy with papers giving latest news,
"All for one cent," with ardor is infused;
He would be *first* to spread about the town
Some murder horrible! — some act profound!
His dirty face, his ragged clothes, bare feet,
Are no embarrassment; for he's a "Greek"
Of "Modern Athens;" and who dare dispute,
His right and title to be Athens *cute?*
He'll hand you papers of an ancient date,
Get his pay and leave you to meditate,
Upon the *sell* your unsuspicious wit,
Hinted to him as a good attic hit.
These boys are haughty, and would dare be *first;*
Loud cry the news, and for high knowledge thirst:
They know that men once shoeless as themselves,
Have risen high by sixes and by twelves;
They know "their country is not yet fenced in;"
That they may swell from Gotham to the Ind.;
Of "Modern Athens," too, that "dear, sweet spot!"
To be of which is well, where'er our lot
Is cast, — whether 'neath the warm tropic sun,
'Mid Russia's snows, or where action was begun.

Thus it is plain that e'en the paper boy,
Is full o' attic *vim* and craves employ,
By which he may ascend the steep of fame,
And write upon its scroll his pauper name.*
He would be *first*, not merely with the news,
But would control the State! and thus amused,
Bethink him how he can his trust abuse,
So that the *people dear*, though Argus eyed,
May not suspect a wrong unrectified.
He is a rascal! — so his foes declare;
But friends, befooled, denounce the charge unfair;
Not *they* believe that such a self-made sage,
Would honor compromise for base 'vantage.
A man of books, he has well learned the way,
Of truth, virtue, — from Plato down to Clay;
His spacious brain by suction has obtained
To know the facts and fancies of each reign,
In each kingdom, since the full, cooling flood,
Cleansed the earth of its early lust and blood;
He's sought to know, and knowing, has perceived,

---

* In thus alluding to the self-reliance, energy, and audacity of those who rise to power by the force of their own wit and gumption, it is not our wish to be understood as being condemnatory of any persons ambitious to rule; for, as we must either lead or follow, it is quite natural that those who have executive ability should desire to gain positions where they can make themselves felt. There can be no objection to this spirit; but there may be a very reasonable objection to the *manner* in which advancement is obtained; and here rests our objection. We affirm, directly and without equivocation, that there is altogether too much *pushing, gouging,* and *fraud* on the part of those who are identified with the material interests of society, and who seek both public and private stations of honor; and we furthermore predict, that unless a higher code of morals obtains, among those who lead in American circles, within the *present* century will begin the breaking up of all government, in this country, which is based — and alone based — upon the general public conscience. When justice becomes obsolete, between man and man, there is no possibility that the idea of liberty, as embodied in our noble institutions, can be maintained and carried out. This is a self-evident proposition, apparent to the most superficial thinker.

The method most judicious to deceive;
He would be *first*, and so he's climbed with care, —
Washed his dirty face, combed his matted hair;
Put on clean linen, clad his bootless feet,
And smiles and smirks, as he may deem discreet.
Thus have we first — the top *knot* of the town —
Your bellowing newsboy, — vender o' popped corn.
All hail, ye ardent workers for high place!
And damned be he who would deny thee grace;
Enter yon dignified patrician's door,
Whence thou 'd been kicked when known as meanly poor;
Look at his daughter fair, just ripe to pluck;
Demand her, sir, and note your wondrous luck;
Take her to thee, and graft upon this stock,
Thine own pure blood! though flowing from a dock,
Or butcher's stall, where nice calves' head and pluck
Are sold for nine-pence, with a goose or duck,
Get the daughter of this most vain, proud sir,
And kill your grease with Lubin's lavender;
Your fame will help to lubricate your name;
And merry goes the day, while rank 's maintained;
But fail, Sir Parvenu! and who can say,
Your wife, so proud, may not put you out th' way,
To gain another, who may chance retrieve
What she hath lost — in thee so much deceived!
Such things *have* happened, where foul " dirt has mix'd
Itself wlth qual'ty;" and a crucifix
Has thus been reared, whereon patrician name,
Has fall'n a victim to the thirst for fame,
Above its reach but snatched by some bold hand,
Rising from nothing to give high command.

In " Modern Athens " — as in noted spots —
The " blooded folks " *will* get mixed with the *outs*;

And when they do, unless these *outs* are " game,"
" The road 's a hard one," and a thorn is fame,
Both 'mong men fighting for its possession,
And with wife at home, — 'gainst her oppression.
" It was a condescension, sir, when I,
The dear loved daughter of Ignatious Spy, —
Whose lineage dates back to, I know not where, —
Consented thus to merge my name so fair,
In that of yours stained with plebean blood,
And ne'er till now 'mong those of honor heard.
Yes, sir, I feel within my veins a fame
Which is above, beyond, your puny name."
So rattles she, this daughter o' the Spys,
Stuffed with foul pride and strangest fantacies;
Her nose is up at all whom she suspects,
Laughs at her nonsense and much disrespects,
Her pretence of blood, and " all that sort o' thing,"
Which brainless egotists delight to talk and sing.
O, we believe in *blood!* we 'd buy a bull,
Or animal of any kind, known to be full
Of healthy blood, and of the soundest stock —
So, too, we 'd deal with man; and, pray, why not?
He is an animal; — has marked this earth
With his tyrant hoof, from its primal birth; —
Marked it with hate, and scorn, and bloody death; —
Tainted the air with his perfideous breath; —
Throttled sweet innocence, and scouted truth,
To serve his baseness, — pander to his mirth.
O, yes, if worth there is to his fallen soul,
W'd put it in a line and let it roll,
Unbroken down from age to age, the gift
Of sturdiest virtue — for 'tis not a myth; —
It *has* a being, though more often found,
'Mong those who aim to *do*, with least of sound.

There are, in " Modern Athens," many flats,
Who talk of blood and noted blooded saps;
And seek by talk to give *their* name a *tone*,
O' honor to which no record can be borne;
They aim by falsehood, and by sheer pretence,
Unmerited to win a consequence;
Rear aloft their heads and think they tower,
With those who wield an *honest* blooded power.
They are heraldic quacks, and should be pushed,
Out of their falsehoods to a better use.
We believe in *blood!* we know virtue runs,
In certain courses as revolve the suns!
That 't is transmitted through unerring law,
To those evolved from out its being's core;
But *they*, all conscious of the gem that 's *their's*,
Boast not its keeping, or its beauty wears,
With haughty brow, but with true dignity,
Unaw'd by snobs or bold vulgarity:
They pass through life most faithful to their trust,
And, as they came, so back return to dust;
If mated they aim to be equal matched,
To live in honor, and to die attached.
These are aristocrats we think of need,
In " Modern Athens " if we would be freed,
From a race of mongrels Jove only knows,
From whom and what they got their " upish nose."
We believe in *blood;* we think it sound sense,
To have faithful record of the source whence,
Our life has come, our morals, and our mind,
To trace distinctly our ancestral line.
It is a good, it is a noble thought,
To be in junction with past ages brought,
" To feel, to see, to know, and to possess,"
The precise lineage of life's progress.

But your pretentious somebody who turns,
A dollar dexterously, oft hurls
Proud airs at those who do not bend the neck,
Because he's rich, and is with mammon decked, —
(Knowing the means whereby he's made a rise,
From some small beer-shop by the force of lies;
Seeing, too, he's got a gaudy coat of arms,
Not his by *right*, but sweet stolen charms,
Taken for *show* on which he "cuts a swell,"
With signet ring, or carriage and a *belle*, —
Some damsel pretty *sold* to him for *gold*,
Whose mind is bounded by her stylish home!
Your "blooded folks," who are indeed a *fact*,
Look on and laugh at this pretentious pack,
Of upstart money-changers who would be,
Kings, in their way, and o'erride gentil'ty.)
They would be *first*, and so they are, indeed;
But last in *true refinement*, cultured breed.
The *potent dollar* in "Modern Athens,"
To all her populace itself commends;
And your fine monied man will e'er be one,
To gather toadies as flies seek the sun;
So he will fancy thus compass'd, carressed,
His worth a treasure and *his* fame the best;
'T is not until he's stricken with a blow,
From fate which stuns him, lays him humbly low,
That he begins to scent how mean a man,
He is to all who knew him in command:
And e'en to those who incense offered up,
To "his great talent," drank his social cup;
But yesterday *first*, to-day *sorrow'd wretch*,
Seeking to borrow — tumbled in the ditch!

Doth see yon slim form, haggered brow, wild eye,

He once was first, and lived expensively;
Gave sumptuous dinners, cracked clever jokes,
And talked most witty with the " finest folks."
He came to Athens when a shirtless boy,
And himself apprenticed in a snob's employ;
The snob was pleased with his cute ready wit,
And put him forward as did best befit,
So smart a chap whose head was hard and clear,
And grasped at once the business o' the year;
Could take a tradesman by the button-hole,
And sell him goods most needed to be sold,
When he, the trader, did not wish to buy,
These things put on him by a wit most sly;
He was a chap who could three columns add
Up, multiply, subtract, divide, and sad
Alone when some shaved fellow broke and paid,
Sixpence on a dollar, and damned all trade:
Of great self-control ne'er was he in wrath,
But kept with nice prudence the pleasant path,
Upward to mingle with Athens' great men,
Punch them in the ribs as one would a friend;
He flourished for a time while " in feather
Full," and out of hard and stormy weather;
But, when the gale did come, " it swept his decks,
Started his timbers," laid him with the wrecks,
Beneath the sea of fortune, where are placed
The lovely, the false, honor, and disgrace.
His wife forsook him, his children turned 'way,
And caused the sire to curse their natal day;
Proud in spirit, quite broken in his heart,
He stands before you in the drunkard's part;
Not as an *actor*, but as the *man himself*,
Who fears to die, though life has nothing left,
To cheer his soul or melt his hardened brow,

Where once was love and joy — all vanished now;
"*The first shall be last, the last shall be first,*"
Saith holy writ! — Athenians, heed that verse;
And, when from circumstance ye are above,
The hard-worked masses, think not to approve
Thy wisdom, or vaunt thyself "born to rule,"
For, e'er thou think'st it, fate may dub thee fool!
Thy trappings costly unto others give,
Once spurned by thee, will never thee forgive.

There dwells in yonder mansion formed of stone, —
Facing the East, — a man of great "back bone;"
A phrase not elegant, but yet approved,
By Young America, that anti-prude;
"He's made up of money" — has lazy sons,
Who sport lazy wives on father's income;
Pass by th' common on any pleasant day,
And you may see these "silken jacks" at play;
Strutting about with canes and knowing look,
As though each head were a well ordered book;
They've little ones, too, and a carriage fine,
Servants to follow — a cellar of wine,
Old as Methuselah — imported for,
Their use alone — mean drinking is a bore;
These are first, though how to earn a dollar,
They do not know, 't is knowledge so vulgar!
Their father's wealth, amassed by rise in lands,
Is so convenient, ready of command,
Why should *they* perplex their "sweet-scented heads,"
And load with cares their now delightful beds?
Why should *they* "with the vulgar rabble mix,"
And turn a penny by th' rule o' three or six?
They don't like to *figure*, save on the road,
At Newport or Nahant, at Rome or Rhodes;

They 're first! *figure else they might come last*,
And with other saps to oblivion pass.
We would not handle roughly these " nice men,"
Who crawl through life as easy as they can;
Yet, we should prove but a careless critic,
To fail to notice their position civic;
They 're first!! they rank among the leading *ton* —
To drink their wine and claim their tongue,
Would be to pass as something more than that,
Which gains you entrance to Mr. Peter Pat's;
For Peter, though a man of generous parts,
Is not a patron of the finest arts, —
That is, he buys a painting now and then,
And " takes a drink " with noble-hearted men;
But he does not pride himself on greatness,
Nor sport a carriage in his kids and best;
He has a wife, but she, good soul is pleased,
To dress in calico, and live at ease;
She *knows* enough; she 'll talk all day with you,
In any language — on *any* subject, too;
She 's not abashed because her husband says,
" Laura, my dear, to me it oft appears,
We 're poor in comparison to those snooks,
With perfumed whiskers and well polished boots."
She laughs, and says, " My darling husband, know
That I, your Laura, with *you* dare to go,
In any presence great soe'er its mine
Of learning, or of trade-begotten coin;
Ideas, my love, *they* are *our* forte, and who
Can outface knowledge or its strength undo;
We may not rank as *first* amid that band,
Of hardened sinners taxed on stocks and land;
But in the wealth of virtue and of soul,
We sum a figure greater than their whole."

Though " Modern Athens " may give loudest praise,
To those who tread successful mammon's ways,
She yet can feel and yet can cherish mind,
That scorns to worship lucre, and to find,
In its sensual pleasure that *keen* joy,
Which many know in having its employ;
She yet can love the student and the man,
Whose soul expansive spurns the trading band,
Of tricky merchants whose sole aim is *gold*,
Getting into place,— gaining the control,
Of material interests which debase,
The heart and its divinity deface;
She yet can feel how noble is that life,
Which asks but little from the world's mean strife,
Of passions poised with deadly aim and scope,
To beat down justice and to o'ercome hope;
She yet can know how noble 't is to be,
A freeman *true — the guard of liberty!*
First, O, first! that is the great, grand idea,
On which " Modern Athens " doth boldly rear,
Its haughty crest steeped in satanic pride,
Which damns all *union, and all hearts divide.**

---

* " In the foregoing vision, I saw everything just as you all will perceive forms and objects, with the penetrating eyes or senses of the spirit, after you have passed away from the body, at physical death. It was very beautiful to see everything clothed with an atmosphere. And in each mineral, vegetable, and animal I saw something of man! In truth the whole system of creation seemed to me like the *fragments* of human beings. In the *beaver* I saw *one* faculty of the human mind; in the *fox*, another; in the *wolf*, another; in the *horse*, another; in the *lion*, another; and so, throughout the entire mass of the spirally progressive and concentric circles of mineral, vegetable, and animal life, I could discern certain relationships to, and indications of, man. Had I then possessed the language, I could have truthfully exclaimed, in the words of the *poet psalmist*,

'Herbs gladly cure our flesh, because that they
Find their acquaintance there.
*   *   *   *
All things unto our flesh are kind.'

Understood in this high sense, how instructive and appropriate was

Tom Jones and Ned Smith were friends till proud Tom,
Was lucky and got a " fine smashing run,
Of paying trade," that gave to him the means,
Of dining on *rare birds*, 'stead of *pork and beans ;*
He's now first! and Smith " may go where he will ; "
Tom's in another sphere, Smith's vulgar still ;
Tom has forgot his friend's an honest man,
Worthy to share *his* luck, with him to stand ;
No, no, that won't do — proud Tom Jones is first,
He's now a Banker, visits Madam *Curse ;*
For *him* to carry up a long tried friend,
Would not be usual, might strangely end ;
Smith might put himself where Mr. Jones would be,
Chief in command, and from all Smiths be free ;
No, no ; to get up among the first is,
Something done which the world greatly prizes ;
Jones can't afford to dispense equalt'y ;
'T would be vulgar — not in conformity
To genteel usage ; and Jones would be true,
To what he deems his new position's due.
Thus may be seen how *snobs* engendered are, —
The warm solicitude and tender care,

Peter's vision (related in the 10th chapter of Acts), in which he saw a great white sheet let down from heaven, containing all manner of four-footed beasts, creeping things, &c., and was told to slay and eat. All this was simply saying thus : — ' Peter, thou needest not feel too exclusive, too partial, too aristocratic, too high minded, and above the meanest of thy fellow-men, nor yet above the little worm that crawls beneath thy feet ; for behold, thou art related to every four-footed beast and creeping thing that the Lord has made. Acknowledge, therefore, thine universal relationships and sympathies, and be lenient to every thing that lives.' There are too many that need Peter's lesson. They, like him, shrink from this new method of tracing out their *genealogy* and ancestral *derivations*, and say they are not used to eating ' unclean things.' But the time is fast approaching when mankind will feel their *oneness* with nature and with nature's God, to the total annihilation of all narrow-mindedness and empty superficiality." — THE GREAT HARMONIA.

They meet from those in sympathy with things,
Of human shape but most inhuman whims!
We sorrow thus to write; — we keenly feel,
Howe'er that *duty* bids us to reveal,
The rot that festers round the heart of life,
And needs the cleansing of th' *dissecting knife.*
We scorn the mean, the coward sneak and fool,
Who puts on airs because 't is his to rule;
We know no honor in the name of first,
'Less *station* is applied to *honor's* use;
If men do toil for power but to press
Dependents, and to jeer at their distress,
We say the time has come when hope is o'er, —
In human love and truth a trust no more.
When, O when, will that happy day arrive,
When right shall triumph, — naught the mind divide!
When man to man shall bear a brother's love,
And seek to do what *conscience* may approve?
When all shall be advanced, — considered first!
And nature cease to groan 'neath Eden's curse.

There are in "Modern Athens" many hearts,
That beat responsive to most gen'rous parts;
We meet them daily in our wonted walks,
And love to ponder o'er their noble thoughts,
Expressed in works that will long point to them,
As nature's true and honored noblemen!
They *are* first! o'er all the world such mind is
Foremost in deeds of courtesy, — with ease
Projecting plans of charity and worth,
To human int'rests o' ev'ry form on earth;
They live for *usefulness*, — to please their God;
To double the talents he did accord,
To them expectant of a full return,

That they eternal blessings shall have *earned*,
From him, the King of kings! above all forms,
Creator vast, whom boundless law informs; —
We meet them in our walks, and feel a pride,
That in "Modern Athens" wit doth abide,
Not pointed merely to the goal of first,
But eager to mitigate th' primal curse, —
To do, to be, in all things great and just,
In sympathy with all, from last to first!
They are first! and tho' unpossessed of *gold*,
Would still be first in purpose and in soul.

Behold that bald, gray-headed patriarch,
In form erect, with eye deep-set and dark;
The "soul of honor," and the pride of men,
He numbers quite full four score years and ten;
Soon must the grave close o'er his earthly frame,
And happier scenes invite to nobler aim,
Than can be followed in this darkened sphere,
Where *change* and *meanness* burden ev'ry year.
Gifted in knowledge, guide of youth and age,
Old Harvard's ex-president, warm friend, sage,
Past-mayor of Athens! whose dauntless will,
Gave her a market; so, too, th' poor from ill,
Shielded with an Ajax' resistless force,
And onward bore the city in its course,
Of new tried government through much of fire,
That passion kindled with a wild desire.
All honor to his mem'ry! o'er his grave,
May roses bloom by th' weeping willow's shade.
Stately in form, with sound and piercing wit,
Th' son is worthy in father's place to sit, —
Ready at dinner with *savans* to blaze,
In th' radiant lustre of ac'demic rays,

Or 'mong men of meaner parts to play,
At bus'ness — from politics to railway:
It matters not to him where he drops in,
He's sure to deal his easy wit and win:
He walks and looks the sense that girts his brain;
In conversation free, in manners plain, —
Honored by Athens, worthy to bear,
His classic name, and father's fame to share.
These are first! and proud Athens knows it too,
Though sometimes lax in giving worth its due.
To such as *these* she owes her note abroad,
The first in all things, — money, pen, and sword!
When merchants cute by artful traffic mount,
High on 'change and hard dollars grandly count;
They should bethink them not in money is,
The awful grandeur *Gas-bag* fancies *his*.
No, no; Gas-bag is befooled, — his success
In trade, or what-not, has so dispossess'd
His better nature (if e'er one he had),
Of generous culture, that his English bad,
Refuses carriage of all thoughts but those,
Which shave the notes alike of friends and foes;
He is so pleased to see his children bow,
To all above him, but no one below; —
Yet, when he thinks he's not *exactly first*,
He damns all trade, — sighs o'er deceptive purse, —
Goes to his God, — kneels in most humble prayer,
For pardon sweet for thinking gold so fair!
And so they go, in "Modern Athens" fine,
Who hope to triumph by jew'lry and wine,
Fine houses, horses, fat wives and girls,
Whose nights are wakeful keeping hair in curls, —
Whose stomachs tender have pouched 'on their hearts,
'Till a lover is as they would a tart,

Or cream, or any other juicy bit,
Of fashionable and taking sweet-meat.
The vainest they of all the fools in town,
Wriggling through the street girt in whalebone,
Or steel, or brass, or substance quite well known,
To shopmen who live by noting o' these first,
That they may learn to ope their tight-closed purse.
Poor things! they want husbands, but mama, pa,
Seek to purchase name shining from afar!
Which doth promise if they could but get it,
A trade superlative — a splendid profit;
They want *their* sons and daughters to mount high,
And though they're first! they ought not to rely,
On their position 'till annexed to those,
Whose blood and brains are equal to all foes.
And so it goes, and so the brassy rich,
Give themselves airs — a certain kind of hitch —
Which 'notes them first, but last in all that's high; —
Above the region of counters, soap, and dye:
They go abroad, in foreign lands to roam,*
When their country's fame bids them stay at home;
Unlettered and untaught in all that's *true*,
They cut such figure as loud peacocks do,
With spread tails on a damp and cloudy day,
With none to applaud their fine vain display;
They hurry off and hurry home content,

---

* It is proverbial, that of the number of Americans who go abroad every year, comparatively *few* are enabled to associate with the higher circles of Europe, with any credit to American culture and manners. We are a nation of money-changers and shop-keepers; and, of course, when thrown into countries where education is thorough, and is a supreme science, our deficiencies are most glaring. It is not that we lack men and women of a high grade of culture (for we have an abundance), but they are not, as a rule, blessed with the means of going abroad; — they have *no goods to buy*, or in any manner are concerned with such business as carries your pushing, gain-loving character into foreign lands.

To have bolted through th' august continent,
Where history points to many noble themes,
And deepest natures lose themselves in dreams.
If they stand in Rome in view of the decay,
Which there is present of her earliest day,
When th' Cæsars' arms bore undisputed sway,
From India's shores to stormy Biscay's bay —
They say, "Why, how strange! I wish I was home,
Where things look *new*, and folks are better known;
I wish I was where I could not see so,
Much of wretchedness and of classic woe;
It grieves me much to feel with time has come,
This gloomy present of tobacco, rum;
And, though I know there's a sort o' glory here,
I must go home, where all things *new* appear;"
They prefer a *freshness* — that's the good,
For which they live, — for which they would be wooed;
And "Modern Athens" doth, through *these* obtain,
In foreign parts, no enviable name;
But they *will* travel, — they're first, and must see,
How people look beyond the dark blue sea;
And then, too, what *are* folks who've not been abroad,
Supped with, or, smelt of, some mean brainless lord?
What *are* folks who can't talk of shaking hands,
With London Cocknies, or Parisian bands,
Of perfumed Gallics, full of toads and rats,
With legs like lobsters, and with eyes like cats?
'T is so delightful to come home and feel,
Raised in the toe — still higher in the heel —
By having brushed up 'gainst these foreign bodies,
Bored to death by swarms of Yankee toadies!
O, money! what a sweet, consoling fact,
To carry *thee*, though heavy to the back,
Since, if we do in all things play the fool,

We yet may "go it,"— yet may claim to *rule!*
And there are those by *scores* in our Athens,
Who, whilst disgusted, yet endure the men,
Whose riches are applied to uses base,
And but for riches would find lowest place,
In social scale to be their proper sphere,
Where vulgar nonsense claims not virtue's tear.

In "Modern Athens" though wealth is supreme,
And they are worshiped who secure its *cream*,
By ev'ry rank, from scholar to bootblack,
Waiting maiden long looking for a Jack,
To mount his back and ride through life a jade
Of note, by spending more than Jack has made!—
In "Modern Athens" though the rich thus bear,
Away the palm of notice and have care,
Bestowed upon their imperial nod, —
They are not quite, though *almost*, near a god!*
What's he? he! why, sir, he's a monied man;
Mark his air, sit not when you see *him* stand;
He holds the kingly purse — is mammon's slave,
Bears chains he courts, as th' battle-field the brave;
Wait on his eye, anticipate his will,
Know that the frown of mammon's slave may kill,
Ay, crush out the heart, darken o'er the brain,
And blast an intellect great in the domain,
Of majestic science which opens to the view,
Th' grand arcana, the beautiful and true,

---

* Our allusion here is to those men, who, upon the bare possession of *money*, assume to be the equals, if not superiors, of scientific and thoroughly educated men and gentlemen. They are individuals who lose no opportunity of turning a dollar, and will have the " pound of flesh " as denominated in the bond. We have no words strong enough to convey our contempt for such specimens of *man*, whom Jesus, when upon earth, found in the temple of the Lord, engaged in *traffic*, from whence he drove them.

Uniting in the essence of that soul,
From which evolved this complex lofty whole;
Yes, oft hath the brutal power of mammon,
Fell like a thunderbolt upon some son,
Of meditative genius and his mind,
Sensitive and haughty and unresigned,
Shattered as some fine kingly forest-tree,
Torn from its earth and cast upon the sea,
To float where'er the restless tide may sweep,
Till lost forever in the mighty deep.
We would soon stay, had we the force required,
This love of riches, *howsoe'er acquired*,
And backward drag the godless hardened mind,
To more of chivalry and less of crime :
We need in " Modern Athens " more of soul,
Which gen'rous culture and high heart enfold : *
The intellect though steeped in classic lore,
Without noble impulse indeed is poor;
" A poor white man," we say, when one of note,
Will Jew his tailor needy on a coat,
Or dine his wife and children off of beans,
While he gets best of wine, rarest birds, greens,
At " crack hotel," famed for its fine larder,
And youths of promise backed by doting father.
Too many of our first are known as mean,
And though quite *attic*, are by no means clean ;

---

* "Thus the prophet inflameth himself, and stirreth up his faith for our example, that we likewise should magnify the blessings and good gifts of God in us, and also our hope and trust in him ; for if the rich men of the world do glory in their *money*, — if they vaunt of their wealth and riches, — why should not we, also, glory in the trust and confidence we have in God, which hath made heaven and earth, — which hath also in his hand all things necessary both for this life and for the life to come ? But because these things are invisible, and cannot be seen but with spiritual eyes, therefore, we commonly neglect them." MARTIN LUTHER.

They like not Spantan broth, yet they would fill,
Their kindred's stomachs with this mess of ill.
For God's sake let us, if we are a class
Of Yankees, which all other men surpass
Be liberal, kind, and with our learning,
Prove our hearts with brother's love are burning.

Love, O, love! that was God's dear gift to man,
When Jesus Christ the Lord, of Bethlehem,
Came in the garb of a mendicant seer,
To teach the doctrine of a brother's tear :
Love, O, love! that is the great need of life,
The only safeguard from remorseless strife.
In " Modern Athens," if we would be first,
Our aim should be to mitigate the curse,
Which came with woman and dwells most with her ;
For e'en now, as erst, she doth sin prefer ;
She must have her love and he must do that,
The serpent whispers beneath her night-cap.
She 'll lay and think and in the morning Joe,
Will have his orders how he is to go ;
Two hundred dollars, or five hundred, as
The case may be is wanted, and she says,
" I 'm a lady, Joe, must dress and visit;
The cash must come from you, or I 'll get it,
From my circle where there 's wit enough,
To prize my charms, and fill my coffers up ! "
So Joe alarmed lest his sweet lady Eve,
Should play the *wanton* and his bosom grieve,
Goes to his office and though " short of funds,"
Sends the amount to dear Mistress Duns.
He thinks himself beloved, but, oh ! how plain,
A tender spot is lodged in his back brain !
And she, this vixen, who has him by the ears,

Sees his weakness — practices on his fears.
O, wedded life! O, love! O, woman *true!*
How sweet to dally and to be with you!
Our fine " Modern Athens " can count by scores,
These dashing females and consummate bores;
Who flount, and flirt, and put on " upish airs,"
Claim to be first — and so they are in cares;
They have so much to think of — babies out
To board — and dressing to travel about,
In all directions to glean the fashions,
And to keep well oiled the wildest passions, —
To play with Dick's whiskers, Harry's sweet lips,
And to pass from ecstasies into fits.
It *will* be so, and men who take to wives,
Bare thus their bosoms to the keenest knives,
That hack and cut for pastime husband's peace,
Though kindly always without stint or cease

We pity men, and yet they get their due,
In " going it blind," when *women* are so few;
Tawdry things there are thick as summer flies,
With padded bosoms and artistic eyes;
They won't work but they 'll marry and exist,
On the hard earnings of " sweet husband's " fist,
So long as stands his dear health and credit;
These gone, and my lady makes a visit,
" Where folks are smart, and can go right ahead,
Without talking poverty — want of bread."
But these are not women — they are beings
Sprung of *fungi*, and with fungi teems.
A woman is a principle! and she,
Is true to her *true* love, *eternally!*
Through sickness and distress — through bliss and woe,
Her heart is constant, — with her *love* doth go!

To lowliest hovel, or to farthest land,
Happy to be where *duty* bids her stand.
We'd trust a *woman!* and we know if bliss,
Upon this sad chaotic earth exist,
'T is only found in her delightful soul,
When linked with one that forms a *perfect whole!*
But the men of "Athens"—some men, at least,
Fail to perceive wherein consists their peace;
And "smashed by a beauty," *got up for sale,*
Put their "foot in," and then the trap bewail:
There's not a party, or a ball, or hop,
Where some *green* swain is not by Nancy got;
She has set her trap she has caught her man,
While lovelier maidens in the background stand;
And as she's caught an eel it is no sin,
She thinks to roast him, or to peel his skin;
At all events she's bound to "eat him up,"
Again set her trap and so on conduct,
Until her heartless days run out and none,
Are found to 'wail the setting of her sun;
She dies and passes to the throne on high,
Of wretched conscience, spurned of Deity!

Oh, "Modern Athens"! would all thy fair knew,
As women wise when well it is to woo!
Let commercial Tom, or bold lawyer Jim,
Attempt with lucre *her* pure heart to win;
And she, untouched by any nobler thought,
Scouts the presumption that *she* can be bought:
Not *she!* she can *love*, but cannot traffic
In marriage — it hath no charm or profit,
In her sweet sense of truth and purity,
Unsanctified by *holy unity.*
When she weds there is resistless power,

By Jove ordained binding to another;
And that union formed in fear and love o' God!
Insures a friendship lasting, deep, and broad;
No storms can shake it no affliction bend,
But she through life is still *devoted friend.*
Delightful woman! thy smile when honest,
Is high manhood's prize chosen as the best!
Thy holy feet through " Athens " daily tread,
And truth's sweet chaplet circles o'er thy head;
Thine eyes are modest and thy mien is mild,
For thou art virtue's dear and saintly child!
Thy vision sweeps eternal life of mind,
And earth doth seem a vapor in its time;
Thy love is not this sphere, nor its vain pomp,
With *thee* is *conscience!* with the eagle mounts,
Thy soaring spirit to the mountain clifts,
Away from heartless, proud, and godless cits:
In *thee* is greatness! thou indeed art *first!*
Above beyond the snobish sneer of purse; —
Money! — what gold can buy thee? what sap win
Thy peerless bosom — thy angelic being?
Cast in a mould — tempered high with brave will,
No snob can bend thee, no fop's beauty kill:
Thou art a *woman!* and " Athens' " *true* men,
Doth love thy influence, and mourn thy end;
The roof that's thine, the grave wherein doth lie,
Thy gentle form are dear to manhood's eye:
Sweet flowers for thee is but sweet to sweet,
Thy grave the spot where virtue's pilgrims meet.

Who then is first, and who is not the *ton,*
May be perceived as we run jingling on.
Thus far we 've said but little of that class,
O' " mutual admirers " led by a man,

Small in stature but great in learned soul,
A dashing scholar, witty, tart, and bold;
He's published books of *rhyme* wherein his face,
Is set with modest and with classic grace;
He's not a *beauty* though an autocrat,
And ties with neatness his nice silk cravat;
Unlike the race of genius he's *precise*, —
Lives by strict rule, and dodges ev'ry vice;
His face is barbered, and his hair is combed;
His feet neat clad, his look is that of home; —
That is, he smacks of having bed and board,
On which he may rely and *can afford;*
In this he's more lucky than wits at large,
Whose home's unstable and whose face is scar'd,
With disast'rous thought and poor blighted hopes,
Of *paying* fame carved out of heavy books!
O, genius! one's heart it doth much of good,
To note our autocrat taking to his food;
To know his stomach though bestirred with thought,
With ease digests clams, pudding, beef, and pork;
He thinks, yet he does it up by *method*,
And wins his laurels though he's not slip-shod;
He honors *Socrates*, but this sage's scorn,
Of soap, water, this modern sage bemournes;
He must have clean teeth, clean shirt, and dicky,
Ere *he* will teach, — be so *very* witty.
Set him at a table where he has been asked,
As first of jokers, large as is the class;
Get him to talk, then give him your ear,
Though small his stature, oh, how "tall" his cheer!
We would like to hit this aut'cratic man,
By way of practice to keep in our hand;
But too good natured he for a roughened steel,
And we'll not stab where conscience would be keen;

Yet must we poke that dear mutual set,
Who none admire, not a fine classic pet,
Or some one who has clambered to the top
Of *getting* — a Greek, so too Hotentot,
By turns as it may be needful to explain,
What knowledge vast one plodder may attain.
We are a friend of learning and approve,
In all staunch healthy brains its ardent love :
Principles are Gods ! and he who works out,
Th' greatest number is stoutest o' the stout ;
Yet that aristocracy of *nice* mind,
Which marks " our Athens," somewhat doth incline,
To *deify itself !* and in finest robes,
To scorn all those who less of science knows.
This insolence is vulgar and that wit,
Who thinks the " mutuals " are only fit,
To come together at the festive board
And elsewhere — deeming that my noble lord,
Is the title due them from the unlettered, —
The wit we say that thus presumes had better,
Unlearn its wisdom, lease itself to *Sam*,
Or some one else, *who 'll bring it out a man !*
Learning is well, but when it puts on airs,
The time has come to tame these haughty bears, —
These animals in ribbons whose tawdry
Heads, are scorched with " fire Greek " and vanity !
Methinks we see some high-flown learned fool,
Viewing the crowd as th' master does his school,
And with self-complacent phiz loud declare,
" What a mass o' ignorance the people are ! "
O Lord ! haste, haste, to Frenchify and Greek
The town, let ev'ry Yankee no more speak,
The good old Saxon — turn at once a calf,
And talk it foreign, and in classic laugh ;

You 'll then be *mutuals* and dine with him,
Who 'll toast you fine and " take you kindly in,"
To admire and praise your expanded wit,
Pleased to be with you — by your side to sit ; —
O, Jesu ! have mercy on the reign of sense,
Ere *all* are students take us softly hence.
We want to learn — we want to idle too,
And keep our fat as healthy farmers do ;
What 's brains without stomach to give them strength,
To bear noble thought and reach goal at length,
Where honor waits patient, where virtue's wreath,
The brows bedeck and holy perfume breathe :
We want to learn, we want to know enough,
To talk with statesmen and with black-skined **Cuff;**
But ambitious as we are we would not,
In seeking learning be a learned sot.
Latin is well, so too is Greek and French,
All is fine kowledge, though not finest sense ;
We 'd add thereto Dutch, Spanish, Italian,
Sanscrit, Hebrew, the tongue of ev'ry land ;
We 'd tack on to this nature's vast expanse
Of facts — a dash of logic — th' mode of **trance ;**
In fine, we 'd tuck the brain so full of *truth*,
That it should be of God the highest proof ;
But then with all our learning — modesty !
Should dwell with us, and ever cherished be.

Ye first of " Modern Athens " in the lore
Of big books, say, are ye not something poor,
In that better knowledge of the kind heart,
That wings no arrow, and that throws no dart ?
If ye form libraries and endow them,
With the master thought of time's noblest men,
Are ye not proud, and crusty, and in naught,

The type of that these gifted authors taught?
Whom ye have placed upon well-loaded shelves,
That youth may garner, boastful as yourselves!*
Be haughty, cold, reserved, and meanly wise,
By true men laughed at, ridiculed, despised.
We would not strike too hard, but our poised pen,
Will not be influenced to release an end,
In truth's imperial cause, God's high praise,
Whose word denounces all in folly's ways.

We cannot forget, we must not pass by,
On learning's record, names not born to die!
The good and great, the truly humble wise,
Whose shades are with us and whose love abides,
Near our hearth-stones to glad each passing day,
And bear in friendship the moments soft away:
They were no fops nor vainest carpet-knights,
Talking of fierce battles but fearing fights;
They *worked* for knowledge, and they knew its worth,
The hard attainment of its priceless truth;
It made them just, and humble, brave and true;
Pleased to *agree*, but stern in *counter view!*
They argued *well*, because their minds were clear,
Their knowledge limpid, bounding as the deer!
They saw the truth, and seized it with a joy,
As marks the cheek of some adventurous boy,
Who saves a life from 'neath the heaving wave,

---

* If we have hit hard at this point, it is because we feel it to be merited. Scholars, as a rule, where there is more than ordinary ability, both in this country and Europe, are stuffed with self-conceit and pride. We may excuse this in the *ignorant*, but in those who have studied the philosophy and the lives of the philosophers of Greece it is unpardonable. What amount of knowledge, we should be glad to know, authorizes a man, or any class of men, to put on airs, and render themselves an insufferable nuisance to all not of the same habits of mind?

And laughing goes to claim a mother's praise:
All honor to such men — urned be their dust,
In "Athens" proud the *humblest*, yet the first!

We would now apply some costic to such,
As talk a deal without informing much;
They are *high-pressure*, and their "boilers burst,"
When they attain to be considered first;
That is, foremost among a certain class,
Where silks, broad cloth, covers many an ass, —
And many a knave decked in finest clothes,
Pooh-poohs at those he now no longer knows:
'T is well, it would be quite unwell if fate,
Should bar these bumpkins vain the name of great.
Mankind are only known as thus they spring,
From close dirty allies into high being!
'T is then we learn how toad-stools may become,
Grand sweeping trees by free unstinted sun.
But let them go — they do but play the part,
Assigned by nature foul — each putrid heart,
Will perish with its day of sunshine warm,
To make more fearful retribution's storm.

Yet ere we leave this dear and perfumed class,
We must not fail to tarry as we pass,
By yonder mansion with high steps of stone,
Where folly revels and where truth's unknown.
It is ——n Street, a fine and spacious walk,
Where maidens gather with trig gents to talk;
It is a street long rented to the mind,
Least stupid and to lofty views inclined, —
It is a street which leads you out of town,
Direct and passes full many a clown,
In gloves, French boots, and slouchy Kossuth hats,

With heads well greased — some-like to whiskered cats.
O, Ammon! how smart these rag-pickers feel,
As by they dash on foot, or with the wheel.
We oft have stood against the iron posts,
To note these mongrels and sum up their cost;
We oft have wondered how in God's name comes,
So many splurgers and so few of duns.
For most wives have! besides score or two,
Of well-kept beauties to arrange their shoe,
If it should pinch and call them dearest dear,
With other nonsense we'll not bring in here.
These perfumed upstarts live — they do, indeed,
And dash the rowels in their ill-used steed,
Hired for the day and driven for the year,
To break up stables with their *smart* career;
They're first in bar-rooms, brothels, and at clubs,
And "play the devil," looking staid as tubs.
But to our purpose of noting those fine
Folks on ———n Street who on rich dainties dine,
And ride 'round "Athens" in their stylish coach,
With foreign dresses and large diamond broach.
First let us look at "dear and sweet mamma,"
Whose face is bloated with a bold *heauteur*;
She seems to say "Thank God I was not born,
To wash up dishes, or to pick a bone, —
Thank God that *I* am *first* and am of blood,
Direct from Noah who battled with the flood;
That *I* at least can boast lineage free,
From butcher's coarseness and base harlotry;
That *I*, of "Modern Athens," bear a name
Equal to any, though not o'ertaxed with fame."
This waddling woman old and vulgar too,
Claims for her *money* what to *worth* is due;
She "puts on airs" and clever shopmen curse,

If they in haste attempt to ope her purse;
Where'er she goes she doth inform the world,
She's Madame *Pride* in the line of earl,
And her hard features steeped in pride and scorn,
Doth threaten death to *villains* unconformed,
To her desires and her imperial will,
Which money founded and gold pampers still.
Her *Dolly* husband stands in awe of wife,
As helpless traveller of assassin's knife;
He walks along through "Athens'" winding ways,
Dunning his tenants — he must "make a raise;"
He's made no deposits for at least two days,
And begins to think 't is much to his dispraise;
Besides his son, the B——, is a bill,
Of expense endless — tending down the hill;
He worked his way to C———'s heart,
And thus in *law's* a son — fine dandy smart!
He treads upon his toes and takes a cold,
From gentlest zephyrs! — on dear life his hold,
Is weak and C——— often sighs,
That he's not out o' the way — since his bright eyes
Have faded! and, oh! she's so fond of change,
She'd fondle puppies in her endless range,
For novelty and all that's *soft* and *new*,
From mush and milk to a sweet apple stew.
Dolly has son of his own ilk but Rome,
Delights him more than his familiar home,
"Where all things are so mixed and men of *birth*,
Are knocked about as though the meanest earth:"
Bah! he would not live at home, no, not *he*;
He hates the Union — its democracy;
A brainless snob! he thinks to be of note,
By going abroad and scorning Yankee vote;
He help to make a President! *he* take

The trouble to our public men create!
The country might explode ere he would do,
A kindness hearty for a base-born crew,
Of grov'lling workers — worthless but to do,
Slave's offices shout their vulgar doctrine,
About equal birth — freedom's offering!"
No, no, your emigrant to "holy Rome,"
Scornes to think of, much less return to home;
He would be where the grandeur of the past,
Looms up in splendor and marked contrast,
With these latter days so tame and vulgar,
That he doth wish the world was rent 'sunder.
So thinks the brother of C——— dear,
Flat as she, and senseless in appear.
The B——— married for a tender home,
For means to dress, o'er foreign lands to roam;
He was a handsome and a well-formed man,
But shiftless as an oyster or a clam;
His glass, his sofa, and his cigar,
Was more to him than all the world by far;
His wife was well enough, but she *would* swear,
And "rip around"— "pitch in" to Sappy's hair;
Until one day poor Sappy thought he'd die,
And leave a world his needs could not supply.
His wife rejoiced and her proud mother laughed,
Papa drank wine and Sappy's *fortune* quaffed!
"There was a time" and such a time we vow,
As ne'er had happened for an age till now;
But no sooner deceased this soft Mr. Jack,
Than hops another *dandy* on their back.
A younger daughter full of senseless love,
Is "smashed" by small talk and a dainty glove;
She weds while our C——— giggles,
For she's grown wise in dear young love's riddles!

She's had her fun and knows what it has cost,
Has had her chills, been nipped by " killing frost ;"
But the younger daughter is left to find,
Out wisdom's narrows with the march of time ;
And break her neck if needful it should be,
To light her out to deep and shoreless sea !
Where " love's young dream " is tossed upon the wave,
Till early wrecked it finds an ocean grave.
O, *these are first !!* king money makes them so,
In their grand train, bulls, bears, and monkies go !
Thus we behold how folly makes its way,
While truth dejected weeps and turns away ;
Thus we behold how poor a thing is pride,
When nonsense spawns it, and when *meanness* guides !
Thus we behold how " Modern Athens " teems,
With flesh and bones formed to petty beings,
Who strut and bluster, sing of *their* great worth,
And crawl like vermin to their native earth.*

But wearied with the *softness* of our theme,
We gladly leave it for some other thing ;
We point to art ! and they who *live* for *it*,
Happy to gain but not bent on profit, —
Unabsorb'd in dollars as the trader, —
They *grasp* not ! but their art's high bliss prefer !
They work for *pleasure*, as much as for coin,
And love those best whose tastes with theirs conjoin.
Artistic genius ! it is a great gift,
From nature and doth on soaring wing lift,
The spirit to nearness with the *Logos*,
Whence came sweet harmony out of chaos.

---

* Some time since the author of this verse was witness to conduct of the most ridiculous character on the part of this family, which suggested the idea of this castigation.

Would "Modern Athens" knew thy gentle love, —
Would raise thee prostrate to a seat above,
The thoughtless rabble whose " bread and butter,"
Three meals per day and extra cold supper,
Is the best good they care to know or aid,
Though challenged to refinement by some maid,
In art whose simple manners skilful hand,
Unite to win the most commercial man;
To teach him fondness for *ideal* commerce,
For forms not *gold* but valued as the *first*,
In purity and all that fills the soul,
With holy pleasure and with self controll;
For *genius* though it may from excess of
Sentiment, lose its balance and befog
Itself in error, yet, those who study
Its pure works, will strengthen their moral force,
And 'scape reefs on which genius 'self is tost!
We speak for art the honor that's its *right*,
We hope for artists something more than night;
Day, bright day *must* come, when they who prize gems
Of genius will true genius' cause defend;
And art in triumph raise to its high place,
Adorned with culture — ev'ry classic grace!
That time *will* come though slow may be its step,
An' many a tear by genius sad be wept, —
Unfed, unhonored, and scornful of life,
Borne down hard pressed by the bitterness o' strife;
Yet will noble art her true sons secure,
From tears and begg'ry when these days are o'er, —
These days of sense, of eating-shops and cooks,
Of wine and bibbling — illustrated books.

And now we pass to science and proclaim,
Her zealous votaries full half insane.

Truth! great Thor! what is it but a two-faced *
Something, a sort of Janus with less grace,
Than an *ourang-outang* and as full of,
Mischief as a fresh virgin is of love.
In *Law* there is no truth of changeless base,
Go to the digests and make out your case,
It matters not how hard a case it is,
Some Lord So-and-so has ruled 't is justice!
By Heavens! 't is enough to make one go mad,
To ponder o'er man's reason dark and sad!
To know how frail the tenure of *all* law,
But holy conscience! God's oracle of yore.
Courts! they are the sloughs of whimsical thought,
Swayed by wild genius for a round fee bought:
Go not to *law* unless you 've a purse full,
Exhausted only by an endless pull.
We are not "down" on lawyers; we know their
Troubles, and with what of consummate care,
They must proceed before judge, jury,
To gain a case and be full up to duty.
But we *are* "down" on the base policy,
Which complicates the law for *larger fee!*
We do not need so much of endless talk
In splitting hairs! we want *clear honest thought!*

---

* Truth in itself, pure and well defined, yields the product of *good*, although in the process momentary evil may be caused. We do not think that *truth*, being the nature of God! should ever be feared; and though we have charged it with mischief, and called it "two-faced," we here speak of it as we note among human societies what passes for truth, or God. As our vision ranges over the world, and peers also into the depths of space, comprehending something of the simplicity of all those beautiful laws by which spirit and matter are equipoised, — the Pythagorean harmony of numbers evolving the music of the spheres; and from this exquisite union of truth and peace, turn to behold the strife, the wretchedness of man, entangled as he is by the errors which seem inseparable from his passions and physical necessities, we feel depressed and humiliated at the woeful contrast, and ask ourself if it is to be thus forever.

The lawyer needs not for his protection,
The mists of logic, if he is a son
Of virtue! and if not he should depart,
From his astute vocation which requires,
A soul of honor and of chaste desires.
In "Modern Athens" there are civilians,
Of noble purpose whom hard cash millions,
Could not, howe'er put in pleasing form, *buy*
To argue 'gainst their conscience or to lie;
All honor to their love of sacred truth,
Their care devoted in dissecting proof:
They *are* first! their holy names shall endure,
In legal forms till records are no more.

We come now to doctors — and, oh, *Mores!*
What birds of prey! e'en from some Doctor Breeze,
Of latter times with his patented pills,
Which cure in one instant all sort of ills,
Up to *Æsculapius* the father
Of physic, pukes, salves, enemas, plaster.
Get sick, and the devil help you! doctors
Wont; some will — a few, but they are bores!
Because the poor they *practice* on,
To be more skillful with the "Athens" ton!
If you want a doctor worth a sixpence,
Be sure to live *well* — with a show of sense,
For he is keen and if he sees no pay,
He'll slight your case, or put you out o' the **way.**
That is the rule! thanks to great Jove! there
Are in med'cine many a name that's fair,
Many a heart that beats with human love,
In sweetest sympathy with highest good,
To man and all pertaining to his fame,
Of being cast the image of that form,

Which guides the light'ning and commands the storm.
They are *first!* " Modern Athens " knows them well,
And ev'ry tongue their deeds of goodness tell.

We pass now to write of that solemn crowd,
Bearing the *cross!* and with deep penance bowed,
Claiming to teach in the Almighty's name,
Yet " living like fighting-cocks " and for fame!*
There 's *some* who live so — with *brains to do it,* —
Those of less talent — without *their* wit,
Must live on husks! and be most circumspect
To live at all — they 're not the people's pet.
And so it goes, and so we 're crammed with *talk*
Theologic — with less of value fraught,
Than would be works, works, mighty works! we say,
That marked the Christians of the early day.
Immortal Jesus! had not where to place,
His God-head with its full, free, boundless grace;
But with his disciples *lived out the truth,*
He came to 'stablish with undying proof:
Whilst those who *now* pretend to do his will,

---

* It is not enough that we have the Gospel, or that we hear it ; but we must believe it, and lay it up in the secrets of our hearts, or we shall not find Christ. God respecteth not the person ; it matters not whether one be learned or unlearned, — instructed in many places of Scripture, or in few ; — unto whom God giveth grace he it is that enjoys Christ. After the wise men had found the child Christ, at Bethlehem, together with Joseph and Mary, by the help of the Scripture and guiding of the star, they were not offended at the low condition of him ; but, being taught by the word, acknowledged him to be the Messiah, the King of the Jews, for whom they had looked for so many years. They then opened their treasures, and offered him gold, frankincence, and myrrh. The wise men do not disdain him because he is without pomp and splendor, neither do they turn back because they find him and his parents in poverty and misery, but undoubtedly acknowledge him as king, as they had learned concerning him out of the Scripture. Moreover, they gave him the honor due to a king ; — they offer him most precious gifts, which they had brought out of their own country.

Are prone to speculate and belly fill,
With all the dainties had through clever pay,
And thus they *vegetate* and Christian *play :* *

> * It happened to us, from a too close attention to books, to break down our stomach, whence ensued cerebral conjestion. In this helpless condition — broken in stomach, heart, and brain — we were abandoned to the resources of our own morbid and chaotic mind. The ministers of "sweet religion" — whose duty it was to be informed of our disease, threatening us with insanity and death — came not near, to soothe, with kind words, our depression and lacerated soul. None but *ourself* was to ourself true. The self-complacent Christian, who knows as little of practical life as a flea does of self-denial, wonders why there should be infidels ; but if they could look with *our* eyes into the Christian ranks, and understand as we do the hypocritical scoundrels, both lay and clergy, who call themselves the church, they would rather wonder why, in the place of one infidel, there are not a thousand. Against the religion of the blessed Jesus we have not one word to say. It is the only light, imperfect as it may appear, by which man can find out the road to happiness, have peace of mind, and be reconciled to his Maker. The many schemes which have been set on foot, from the earliest records of speculative philosophy, explains nothing, but leaves the mind darker than before ; with none of Christianity's magnificent hopes, supported by the blessed spiritual convictions of their reasonableness. Yet the arguments of the opposers of Christianity have a strength we could wish otherwise ; the most potent of which is that Christians themselves do not carry out in practice their professions ! This, alas ! is too true, in too large a number of instances. The *spiritualism* of Jesus is the most perfect ever given to the world. Rightly understood and followed, this existence, instead of being a snare to so many, would be a *bearable* condition ; and instead of remarking as we do, upon the human countenance, from early life to old age, such terrible marks of evil passion, and confusion of ideas, we should see there nothing but an honorable conscience, sustained by the Holy Ghost, which is the influence of Christ extended to all those who believe in, and *practice*, his conciliatory and self-sacrificing spirit. We regret to be able to say that the writings of the early fathers are so contradictory in regard to the teachings of Christ and his apostles, and that the Bible itself is so confused in its text, that no positive knowledge as to what was actually spoken by Jesus, and commanded by him to be believed, can conscientiously be avowed. And it does seem, to any other than one of the greatest imaginable faith and humble intelligence, quite incredible that God should have submitted, through the person of Christ, to so much indignity from man, to redeem him, and yet preserve no more satisfactory record, to all minds, of his will and teachings, than we now possess, or are likely to possess. The theological jargon which passes for religion, among so large a number, is but a poor apology for the fact that 't is the best truth that can be found. Yet, despite the deceptions, disingenuine-

They are more of deists than of sweet Christ;
This world's their home — here's their sole Paradise:
We mark them on the street — in the pulpit,
With less of piety than worldly wit;
They theorize, and speculate, and damn,
With sceptic notions the quiet of the land.
Out of that church with error blackened o'er,*
The mother of ages! and the "great whore,"
There is no peace but all to discord tends,
And man with man in subtlest thought contends.
The Romish priest though packed with holy lies,
Holds to his doctrine and for religion *dies ;*
The heretic pastor if unshackled,
(Though not compelled for proud Rome to battle),
Is stuffed with *novelties* and knows not what,
Is safe to preach to people, or what not:
He seems to lack authority! and men
May hear him earnest teach, but, oh! what then?
Others there are *as earnest* who declare
All is falsehood, that Christ was but a seer, —
A man like other men, — a noble soul,

---

ness, and hypocrisy of the clergy, who insist upon retailing from the pulpit their scholastic nonsense, and despite the *innocence* of large numbers, who are charmed with their instruction, we are free to hope that the little that we do know of Christ will, ere long, be fairly stated, and the world be put in possession of *the truth, the whole truth, and nothing but the truth.* We think upon such a basis a religion may be established that will command the attention of men, and influence their action.

* In alluding to the subject of religion, in connection with the Roman Catholic Church, we felt bound to award that most remarkable power the credit which is its due, while at the same time we perfectly well know it is without any valid claims whatever to have proceeded either from Jesus Christ or his apostles. It is a sheer invention of man, to control by the trappings and insignia of power the self-willed masses; and as a means to such an end, it worked admirably to the time of Luther, and yet continues to wield an immense influence. We are an enemy to the institution, because it is an unqualified cheat, designed by knaves.

Who sought the good from out this wicked world,
Appealed to his Father as we also,
May pray and e'en as Christ the Father know.*

* In the Gospel of St. John (chap. 3) is plainly and directly shown the difference of the persons, in the highest and greatest work that God accomplished for us poor human creatures, in justifying and saving us; for there it is plainly written of the Father, that he loved the world, and gave to the world his only begotten Son. These are two several persons, — Father and Son. The Father loves the world, and gives unto it the Son. The Son suffers himself to be given to the world, and " to be lifted up on the cross, as the serpent was lifted up in the wilderness, that whosoever believed in him should not perish, but have everlasting life." To this work comes afterwards the third person, the Holy Ghost, who kindles faith in the heart through the Word, and so regenerates us, and makes us the children of God. This article, though it be taught most clearly in the New Testament, yet has been always assaulted and opposed in the highest measure; so that the holy evangelist, St. John, for the confirmation of the article, was constrained to write his Gospel. Then came, presently, that heretic, Cerinthus, teaching out of Moses that there was but one God, and concluding hence that Christ could not be God, or God man. But let us stick to God's word, in the Holy Scriptures, that Christ is true God, with God the Father, and that the Holy Ghost is true God; and yet there are not three Gods, nor three substances, as three men, three angels, three sons, three windows, &c. No: God is not separated or divided, in such manner, in his substance; but there is only and alone one divine essence, and no more. Therefore, though there be three persons, — God the Father, God the Son, and God the Holy Ghost, — yet notwithstanding, we must not divide or separate the substance; for there is but only one God, in one only undivided substance; as St. Paul clearly speaks of Christ (Colos. chap. 1), — that he is the express image of the invisible God, the first-born of all creatures; for through him all things are created that are in heaven or on earth, visible, &c., and all is through and in him created, and he is before all, and all things consist in him. Now, what the third person is, the holy evangelist, St. John, teaches, chap. 15, where he says, " But when the Comforter is come, which I will send unto you from the Father, the spirit of truth which proceeds from the Father, he shall testify of me." Here Christ speaks not only of the office and work of the Holy Ghost, but also of his substance and faith: he goes out, or proceeds from, the Father; that is, his going out, or his proceeding, is without all beginning, and everlasting. Therefore the holy prophet Joel gives him the name, and calls him, " the Spirit of the Lord." Now, although this article seems strange or foolish, what matters it? It is not the question whether it be so or no; *but whether it be grounded on God's word or no*. If it be God's word, as most surely it is, then let us make no doubt thereof; he will not lie; therefore let us keep close to God's word, and not dispute how Father, Son, and Holy Ghost can

"Modern Athens" is stocked with infidels;
They are first! and important station fills.
They deify the intellect! and think
The soul is competent to approach th' brink,
Of that eternal truth which dwells with God, —

be one God; for we, as poor wretches, cannot know how it is we laugh, or how with our eyes we can see a high mountain ten miles off, or how it is that when we sleep in body we are dead, and yet alive. This small knowledge we cannot attain unto; no, though we took to our help the advice and art of all the wise in the world, we are not able to know the least things which concern ourselves; and yet we would climb up, with our human wit and wisdom, and presume to comprehend what God is, in his incomprehensible majesty! The chief lesson and study in divinity is that we learn well and rightly to know Christ, who is therein very graciously pictured forth unto us. Christ himself teaches that we should learn to know him only out of the Scriptures, where he says, "Search the Scriptures; for they do testify of me." St. John says, "In the beginning was the Word, and the Word was with God, and the Word was God." The Apostle Thomas also calls Christ God, where he says, " My Lord and my God." In like manner St. Paul, 9th Romans, speaks of Christ that he is God! where he says, " Who is God over all, blessed forever! Amen." And, Colos. 2, " In Christ dwelleth all the fulness of the Godhead bodily;" that is, substantially. Christ must needs be true God, seeing he through *himself* fulfilled and overcame the law; for most certain it is that no one else could have vanquished the law, angel or human creature, but Christ only, so that it cannot hurt those that believe in him; therefore, most certainly he is the Son of God, and natural God. Now, if we comprehend Christ in this manner, as the Holy Scripture displays him before us, then certain it is that we can neither err nor be put to confusion; and may then easily judge what is right to be held of all manner of divine qualities, religions, and worship that are used and practiced in the universal world. Were this picturing of Christ removed out of our sight, or darkened in us, undeniably there must needs follow utter disorder; for human and natural religion, wisdom, and understanding cannot judge aright and truly of the laws of God; therein has been and still is exhausted the arts of all philosophers, of all the learned and worldly-wise among the children of men. For the law rules and governs mankind; therefore the law judges mankind, and not mankind the law. If Christ be not God, then neither the Father nor the Holy Ghost is God; for our article of faith speaks thus: " Christ is God, with the Father and the Holy Ghost." Many there are who talk much of the Godhead of Christ, as the Pope, and others; but they discourse thereof as a blind man speaks of colors. Therefore, when I hear Christ speak and say, "Come to me all ye that are weary and heavy laden, and I will give you rest," then do I believe stead-

> To share with *Him* the glory of His nod!
> Blasphemous insolence! what is the mind,
> That it should thus its puny self *sublime?*
> What has it learned with all its boasted wit,
> Since Eden's day that doth a God befit?

fastly that the whole Godhead speaks in an undivided and unseparate substance. Wherefore, he that preaches a God to me that died not for me the death on the cross, that God will I not receive. He that has this article has the chief and principle article of faith, though to the world it seem unmeaning, and even ridiculous. Christ says, "The Comforter which I will send shall not depart from you, but will remain with you, and will make you able to endure all manner of tribulations and evils." When Christ says "I will pray to the Father," then he speaks as a human creature, or as very man; but when he says I will do this or that, as before he said I will send the Comforter, then he speaks as very God. In this manner do I learn my article, "That Christ is both God and man." Let whatever will or can befall me, I will surely cleave by my sweet Saviour Jesus Christ; for in him am I baptized. I can neither do nor know anything but only what he has taught me. The Holy Scriptures, especially St. Paul, every where ascribe unto Christ that which he gives to the Father, namely, the divine almighty power; so that he can give grace and peace of conscience, forgiveness of sins, life, victory over sin, and death, and the devil. Now, unless St. Paul would rob God of his honor, and give it to another that is not God, he dared not ascribe such properties and attributes to Christ, if he were not true God; and God himself says, "I will not give my glory to another." Isa. chap. 42. And, indeed, no man can give that to another which he has not himself; but, seeing Christ gives grace and peace, the Holy Ghost also, and redeems from the power of the devil, sin, and death, so is it most sure that he has an endless, immeasurable, almighty power, equal with the Father. We must think of no other God than *Christ.* That God which speaks not out of Christ's mouth is not God. God, in the Old Testament, bound himself to the throne of grace; there was the place where he would hear, so long as the policy and government of Moses stood and flourished. In like manner he will still hear no man or human creature but only through Christ. As numbers of Jews ran to and fro, burning incense and offerings, here and there, and seeking God in various places, not regarding the tabernacle, so it goes now: we seek God every where; but not seeking him in Christ we find him no where.

MARTIN LUTHER'S "*Table Talk.*"

In regard to the doctrine of the Trinity, we wish to be understood as expressing the opinion that it is *possible* it may be true. We cannot, with Luther, maintain that it *is;* because we know the question to be beset with the most profound and unhappy difficulties.

What knows it compared to what's yet unknown,
Eternal space where widest systems roll!
And shouldst presume to doubt it may be so,
That Christ was God! — that we can only know,
Of spirit and its peace through *his* high word,
Erst in Judea and by Jordan heard?
O, no, the mind of man is not of force,
To come to God through reason's slipp'ry course!*
The world had tried it, and had tried in vain,
When Christ appeared in great Jehovah's name!

---

* We are pained to state that in our judgment the *clergy*, as a body, are far from being true to their exalted mission. Whoever has familiarized their minds with Christianity in the apostolic age, as it is presented by Mosheims and other able, candid, and impartial writers, must look with supreme contempt upon large numbers of " God's servants," in these degenerate times, who discourse of politics, and nearly all the extraneous matters of the day, to the exclusion and scandal of true Christianity. *These clerical villains are the scourge of the times;* the willing instruments of *Satan*, in the work which is now being consummated of universal hate, consequent on the overthrow of the idea of self-government as expressed by our political and social institutions. No man, in his right senses, can fail to perceive that the clergy have had much to do in the production of the wild and godless fanaticism, which, being a *religious faith!* can only be silenced and exterminated by the sword of an avenging wrath in the bosom of those men, who, inspired by a hearty common sense, and a magnanimous conscience, are ever ready to do battle in defence of practical ideas, that redound most to the honor of God, and advance most the general interests of his creatures. We charge upon an apostate, vile, and villainous pulpit much of the growth of that hostility to the slave interest at the South, which nothing, in our judgment, can now remove but the direct interposition of Heaven. It seems to us that if the South are true to themselves, — steadfast to their honor, — that, rather than be governed by a Northern party, of declared enmity to its great and leading interest, she will incur any risk, however fearful, in repudiating the Constitution. That such will be her action admits not of a doubt; and that she will have the sympathy of Christendom, in support of her honor, is equally certain. We trust the *Union* may be preserved. We are indeed strong *united*, and have a momentum of surprising force, in marked contrast with that condition which would follow dissolution and the business of civil war and bloodshed, such as we have no record of in the annals of time, deep with gore as they are; but this preservation of so great a legacy must depend upon Northern justice and valor.

He spoke, and perished! but his word will live,
To cheer the helpless as they silent grieve.
In "Modern Athens" those men are the first,
Who accept the " mean doctrine " of the curse,
And preach repentance of our daily sins,
Obtained through Christ with whom our life begins,

And now we turn to that audacious pack,
Of brazen reprobates who 're labeled " quack,"
In art and science, in ev'ry phaze o' life,
They cut large figure, rampant in the strife.
They 've bought up all th' papers with their custom,
And editors of course are cautious — *mum!*
They 'll let them gull the public to a man, —
They pay the price, " the public may be hanged."
We like ability in any form,
Whether to patch an eye or cure a corn;
But when sound learning and still sounder sense,
Is starved to death by *quackish impudence*,
We think the time has come to seek a plan,
To gibbet quacks, and fumigate the land.
There 's Doctor So-and-so who pulls out teeth,
And Lawyer So-and-so with his stout brief, —
There 's Parson John pounding hard the pulpit,
Exciting sinners to laughter, or a fit;
There 's your surgeon bold with his knife stuck in,
To some poor patient's tough and greasy skin;
There 's your man o' physic o'er a lady's breast,
Ambling with her mouth to find out her distress;
There 's a fellow, hard driving a split pen,
Ambitious of shining 'mong lettered men;
There 's a crack-brain with chisel or a brush,
Who thinketh art *his* mission — *he* the first
Of artists! — weeping that the " unkind world,"

Should squibs and laughter at his labor hurl ; —
All *quacks!* there's not a " mother son " without,
The gift of doing what they know 'naught 'bout!
A clever talent this we must admit,
But not akin to honest common wit,
And should be cuffed and kicked till it withdraws,
From those high seats grasped by its dirty paws.
Yet *quacks* will flourish, since many persons are,
More pleased with humbug than with truth by far:
They love to be deceived! and he who can,
Please their fancies is much the better man.

The *student* now doth claim our wand'ring eye,
As he with patience does thought's lens apply ;
Forgetful oft that he has a body,
In his ardent love of books and study.
In " Modern Athens " there are numbers who,
Are curious and seek extensive view ;
They've ransacked all ages and can relate,
The reign and crimes of every potentate ;
They seem to live more in the distant past,
Than in the brief present with its mean cast,
Of incident compared with what has been,
When glory moved all hearts and great was king.
We love the student for his labor tells,
O' one who follows not the beaux and belles ;
Whose head is thoughtful and whose heart is pure,
Who honors truth! delights to hunt it o'er.
And though his brains may not forever be,
Able to attain th' truth successfully,
So mixed with error is it yet his work,
Is noble and without least taint of hurt ;
And if he bears within his soul the will,
To conquer error he may thus fulfil,

A mission high and live a happy man,
Conscious of God — led of *his* holy hand.
Study is well, so too is gentle play,
The one should follow as the night the day:
They are first who in earnest seek the truth,
If feet are large and patched may be the boot.
In " Modern Athens " the studious man must,
Ever be held esteemed among the first;
To know, to be, a lexicon of facts,
Is e'er to mount and ride on others' backs.
Get knowledge if thou would be known as first,
The only terror to commercial purse, —
The mere money-king who waves oft his hand,
In token bold of his astute command, —
With *learning!* thou may'st cool him down to *one!*
Make him respectful as a well-whip'd son.

But what of lit'rature, of those who *read*,
And dear publishers and authors feed,
Sometimes with silver spoon, then one of *brass*,
Which gives 'em canker — oh! 't will be the last,
Effort for an age to please a dull set,
Of book-worms who read only to regret,
Their time and money does not *yield much more*,
With stomachs weak and eyes so painful sore.
Yes, the publishers with some thousands out,
And authors who are grumbling with the gout,
Are " down " upon " blue stockings " and slim legs,
Owned by gents who walk only to their beds.
But what care readers! they say they are *first*,
And must be served, or publishers will burst.
And so it goes; your reader is a lord,
In " Modern Athens " as he is abroad;
Pleased he *must* be, or his dimes will remain

In bank, and bookstores soon run short of change.
There 's something quite amusing in readers,
Who snuff and do not snuff — " they are sneezers " !
There 's not a single one from Bess to Ralf,
" That is not thunder " in learning's high behalf;
It matters not whether they 're learned in signs,
Have drank the classics up, or Flemish wines ;
They 're readers ! and that, sirs, is quite enough,
They 'll damn your trade if you 're not " up to snuff."
By Heavens ! 't is a lovely sight to see,
These readers on a literary spree ;
They 've got several new books ; " and what can,
Be said new at all by earthly man ? "
That 's the great question ! look out for breakers,
O, authors ! when thy lamp-scented papers,
Have been devoured, and their flat taste discussed,
Which some laugh at, whilst others they disgust !
They are *readers*, sir, and their opinions,
Thy law is ! ye are their booted minions !
If you don't think as they would have you think,
The devil grim may take you in a wink.
In " Modern Athens " there is no class so,
Confident — ready with how much they know !
One can tell these readers at a glance,
They bear within their eye wit's bluntest lance ;
They walk too as though they bore on their top,
The " cream " of each heavy publisher's shop ;
And yet, too often, should we tap their head,
Their vast attainments bright would be but lead !
There is a difference 'tween the student,
And the *reader* merely — one is bent,
On stuffing orderly and well his brain,
With what he proves to be decided gain ;
The other like a *lap-dog* would be *pleased*,

And seeks to know with the most perfect ease.
Books are to him what lovers are to maids, —
Footballs to kick when fickled mood persuades.
Authors, we pity you! we feel your woe,
To be thus exercised by readers' toe;
Yet *there is no escape* — you 're after *fame,*
And you must pay the price of honored name!
If kicked, be patient! let them kick again;
You 've got your library — you 've got your pen,
And you 've got your publisher — that 's a bore,
Harder than all with *patience* to endure;
For, if you 've *genius* but have got no " tin,"
They 'll print your musings, and they 'll " put you in."
For *sixpence!* to their fat, full-faced dollar!
Howe'er hard you grunt, and groan, and holloa.
But publishers are well enough — they 're first,
In " our Athens " when not by *readers* cursed.
And of all men the *author* is the last;
A bootblack, a scavenger, a jackass,
Are they dependent for their daily bread,
On what may chance to rattle in their head;
And what may chance to fit a bookman's trade,
To please a loafer or to tease a maid.
Genius, — poor genius is the last to see,
Itself rewarded and from sorrow free!
But though ye thus do suffer and thus weep,
Thy soul is mighty and thy thought is deep.
If man will not a proper homage pay,
But leave thee lonely to pursue thy way,
Thy scorn is fire and thy heart is iron,
The world thy laughter, cherished dreams *thy* sun,
Brighter far than the light which doth illume,
Those darkened bosoms, that false pride assume,

Who would have thee work, see thee die of want,
And mourn thy exit with a tender grunt.

The critic now doth offer to our hand,
Attempting oft with "faintest praise to damn;"
We've seen such fellows, and we've seen them whip'd,
By something less than classic school-boy wit;
They've great courage when they scent no danger,
Snappish and snarling as th' dog in th' manger;
But let a crack of genius sharp the ear
Arrest, and they fall backward in the rear;
They're last just now, but will quite soon be first,
When some moderate author comes with verse;
They'll "shin" *him* sure, and if his bones are loose,
They'll shake them out of him with mean abuse.
In "Modern Athens" these quill-men are first,
When they *dignify* not *abuse* their trust;
But most strange it is we have few critics,
Who are superlatively diamond wits;
They may *well* cut, but they do not *sparkle!*
Their knife's a bowie — not an article
Of finished poignancy which does its work,
With thoroughness! but not with *lasting hurt!*
We want *such* critics, we must have them too,
Fair play to *authors* is from "Athens" due.

One word of clerks! those small and tender limbs,
Of commerce whose labors with day begins;
Whose pay's a trifle and whose hopes are dark,
Whose life's a burden, and whose bliss a spark,
No sooner kindled than fate puts it out,
Through churlish master or some other lout;
They are but *clerks*, and pray what is a clerk,
More than common and most neglected dirt?

They help make fortunes, but well what of that,
The mule draws th' dray, the soldier bears the 'sack;
But neither mule or man is thought to be,
Worthy of care in any marked degree;
They are driven fast or slow as the need,
Of master may require, and though they bleed
At heart, and ask whence has sweet justice flown,
Echo responsive greets them with a moan:
And so they pass and " onward plod their way,"
Till " worked to death " they back return to clay;
Glad to depart from out the traces drear,
In which they've pulled unloved from year to year;
In which they've known how base it is to serve,
Where honor is not and where truth's unheard!
Take courage clerks! and if thy talents are,
For others plied be thou above them far;
If they thy talents use and do not give,
Thee recompense to *save* as well as *live*,
Above them be in this, accomplished mind!!
A bliss they know not with their much-prized coin:
Teach them to feel there is a solace dear,
In cultured taste though oft flows sorrow's tear;
Teach them to be, though masters, *gentlemen!*
To pay for service what 't is worth to them.
Let thy example and thy spirit brave,
Teach them thou art no mean and coward slave;
That thy soul is lofty, thy purpose pure,—
Equal with them before God's perfect law;
So shalt thou stand 'mid " Athens " honored first,
Humble though thy lot, scanty though thy purse.

And last, not least, in our love, *mechanic*,
We take thy hand and have pleasure in it;
Thy " bone and sinew and thy manly brain,"

Are "Athens' " boast, and "Athens' " needful gain!
There is a set who turn their backs on thee,
But *manly* hearts of insolence are free!
'T is only those with more of pride than sense,
Who fail to see thy foremost consequence;
The knowledge which is thine, and must be thine,
To do thy labor taxes much thy mind;
Not more the merchant or the physician,
Stout manhood needs to maintain *position!*
When thou art true to thyself and science,
Thou art the *first*, howe'er unrecompensed
May be thy weary toil while others play,
And strut about as idlers all the day:
We trust the time's not distant when thy mind,
Will more of *right* in mammon's conscience find;
When thy pay shall be worthy of thy toil,
Thy hand no meaner 'cause that it is soiled.
It is to *thee* " our Athens " owes her dress,
Of mechanic beauty! her happiness
In fame! thy "vulgar energies" conjoined
With *capital* hath wafted o'er the main.
And shall *thy* solid worth be trampled on,
By upstart pigmies to starve perhaps anon!
Looking as though a stout hammer and nail,
Would spend their wind and flat their spreading sail.
Are such as *these* to outface thee brave man,
In "Athens" noted for thy most skilful hand!
Oh, no, thou 'rt first! hold up thy honest head,
And be not dashed by peacock pigmies' tread.

And now to close; yet ere we wipe our pen,
And bring this doggerel to a speedy end,
We would discursive wander through the town
And turn a few more sweet " Athenians " round:

First, there is Jim munching his dime cigar,
Great at billiards, and often at the "*bar.*"
He loves the ladies, but their papas say,
To win so *smart* a youth will never pay.
He's first!!! that is, his family is known,
To live about the lofty State House dome;
He's a gymnast smart, can box well and fence,
In these accomplishments he shows much sense.
Then there's Titans! who'll *oar* it full two miles,
Ere you can kiss a maiden for her smiles.
They are trumps! and only play to win,
Loving a boat as Satan worships sin:
But with all their muscle, oars, and prizes,
They are modest youths and wait on ladies;
They are not "blowers" though heroes bold,
In "Athens" honored for their manly soul:
We think them first — we think all fully first,
Taking to water — and who take the *purse!*
We bid God speed heroic *muscle* — mind
Too, that loves th' oar, but not to oars incline.

From hearty youth we pass to proud old maids,
Decked out in crinoline and in brocades;
They've had more offers than pet squirrels nuts,
But *their* "dear men" have been misfortune's butts,
Who would not wed "till they could see their way,"
For honor bade them keep dear love at bay.
So thus these maidens once so fresh and fair,
Have been compelled a lap-dog for an heir;
They "rip out" sometimes, but when day is fine,
And the heart beats freely as runs good old wine,
They get up a laugh and wonder how 't is,
Girls are so pleased with man's disgusting phiz.
They would not marry the best one alive,"

Though bad their teeth, their hair most deeply dyed.
They sigh to think it though, for after all,
There is joy in whiskers nicely oiled;
They feel so down-like laid gently on the face,
While husband's arm enfolds the wife's dear waist,
That really, though men are plagues and puppies,
Pleased they would be with *some*, at least, as wooers.

There are in " Modern Athens " men of note,
Who 'bout theatres, show-shops, and bar-rooms float;
They are the " small-beer wits " who croak, splutter,
Of genius and bet high on one another;
If they can make their bed, and board, and drinks,
'T is all they care for — " damn what th' parson thinks;"
With managers, editors, reporters,
They are arm-in-arm as sons and daughters:
Their smiles are mutual and their hearts soft,
As hides in store-house on Commercial Wharf.
Perhaps wooing the manager is one,
Who's got a play he would have speedy done;
The " manager dear " loathes him in his soul,
But as 't is genius pleads he must out-hold,
Some look of kindness and with base pretense,
Appear to honor his dramatic sense.
And so it goes, and so those who would gain,
From out the stage an author's noble fame,
Must write his scenes with trembling and in fear,
To be repaid by disappointment's tear;
To be kicked and pushed by actors and pimps,
Who beset our theatres like deathless imps.
If one has genius to write classic play,
He *gold* should have to pave his muddy way,
To keep himself aloof from meanest pack,
Who labor hard to break an author's back.

Money, ay money, is the need of all,
The drama's genius as the "nigger's ball;"
If you have mind and soul and will to be,
A noted character — be banker! — he
Can have plays done though poor their plot and sense,
Buy managers, actors, with recompense!
Let lubbers howl their criticisms wild,
What care thee — fortune's imperial child! *

The stage should be held in the highest praise,
"Nature's mirror" in each succeeding age!
Genius alone should govern and control,
And favors asked should be denied the bold,
And pert who forward push to fill the place,
Which genius most godlike alone can *grace!*
We know 't is easy to define the law,
That should prevail as it prevailed of yore,
When men were authors whose wild stormy souls,
Demanded actors equal to their *roles!*
And actors too were men whose genius felt,
The glow of nature and with transport melt!
Who soared with no hand — op'd no mouthing lip,

---

* We have no hesitation in saying that the manner in which the favors of managers, actors, and actresses are obtained, by those wishing new pieces produced, is a sad stigma upon the profession. An author, or his friends, must play the *toady* for an indefinite period, or possess such an overshadowing influence as to *command* their support at once, in order to get a new piece performed, which, if successful, imposes upon the "poor author" an everlasting debt of gratitude, he is not expected ever to be able to pay. If his plays make him anything, and he does not give pretty much all to those who have performed it, his *meanness* becomes the subject of general discussion; so that a man, unless under the most favorable circumstances, had better at once hang himself, than attempt to acquire either fame or a competence by *dramatic authorship.* He is beset on all sides by enemies, among whom are a dissatisfied pack, who have the ambition to write for the stage, but neither the talent, genius, or industry to accomplish anything meritorious. They block the way of true merit, as so much immovable lumber, and are an unqualified nuisance!

Whose form and features were a language fit,
To bring down the house — fill the eye with tear,
Winning nightly laurel from " the public dear."
But though that age has passed and at this hour,
The drama crippled has lost its power,
Yet may it be in " Modern Athens " made,
To flatter genius and its merit aid;
There is no school like *it*, and people will
Cherish its love and cling around it still;
The poet's soul exhales most fragrance here,
Which nature counterfeits to virtue rear:
Let " Modern Athens " place among her first,
The drama's masters of the sock and verse,
Let this art so ancient and truly great,
Be here protected from disastrous fate;
Let it be raised at once and all become,
Pledged to guard it even to martyrdom.

And now, kind reader, be thou foul or fair,
We thank thee warmly for thy 'tentive ear;
If thou perchance doth deem we've stricken hard,
Bethink thee of our subject — that the bard,
Is privileged to speak the truth though sad
Its telling, when listeners would be glad.
If life is sickening and if mankind,
Prefers *clouds* to *light*, to continue blind,
We are not disposed to aid in this
Oblivion — to greet them with a kiss,
When we should reprove and dare to inform,
Of what we see in human life deformed;
If we write and publish, ye shall perceive
As we, the great, and oh, most crying need!
Of sense and virtue 'mong the class who reign,
Above the censure and the breath of blame;

But we can reach them with our trusty pen,
And though not Jove, we yet can *truth* defend!
It is the only cause on this tear-wet earth,
Worthy of manhood's love and manhood's work!
It is the only cause which moves the heart,
Towards its God, and godlike strength impart!
Forgive us, then, if in our hearty hate,
For those tawdry beings *who would be great*,
We have thrown our ink with ungentle force,
To stay mad folly in its wayward course.

Farewell, our friend! if indeed thou 'rt a friend;
We wish thee merry to life's latest end;
And when thy bones shall repose in the box, —
As thou art laid in th' tomb with other corpse, —
May thy spirit freed from care, passion, here,
Be perfect honor in a nobler sphere;
May virtue's laurels bind thy angel head;
Thy prayers be offered for the coming dead;
And if, perchance, our steps thou dost precede,
Attend our sorrows and supply our need;*
So we will part, and in that parting hope,
On *truth* hereafter to more fondly *dote*.

---

* "There is something, I am convinced," continued Byron, "in the poetical temperament, that precludes happiness, not only to the person who has it, but to those connected with him. Do not accuse me of vanity because I say this, as my belief is that the *worst* poet may share this misfortune in common with the best. The way in which I account for it is, that our imaginations being warmer than our *hearts*, and much more given to wander, the latter have not the power to control the former; hence soon after our passions are gratified, imagination again takes wing, and, finding the insufficiency of actual indulgence beyond the moment, abandons itself to all its wayward fancies, and during this abandonment becomes cold and insensible to the demands of affection." — *Lady Blessington's Conversations with Byron.*

"*Species ducet te, video.*"
HORACE.

NOTE.

If any one should have the patience and good nature to read through this rhyme, and, after "due deliberation," should charge the author with a "base and malicious disposition towards the wealthy classes," he has only to say to that person, whoever he or she may be, that he values such an opinion as he does the howling of a wolf chained to a pig-sty. There is no one who entertains a higher regard for *honorable* wealth than he. A good and liberal, whole-souled man, cannot have too much of this world's goods ; because he looks upon his success as a trust from Heaven, and aims to discharge his duty faithfully. These and their wealth he highly esteems, whether he happens to be the recipient of their friendship or not.

His rhyme has been directed against those miserable wretches whose money is their god, — whose puffed-up, vain, and conceited souls are incapable of a noble impulse, and the chief pleasure of whose lives appears to be, "looking down" on their less fortunate fellow-citizens, and assuming a consequence which is as contemptible as it is vulgar, and unauthorized either by common sense or common honesty.

If his rhyme offends these snobs, he thanks God they are capable of feeling his arrows, and he only regrets it is not in his power to drive them between the watery walls of some Red Sea, that like Pharoah and his host, they and their bastard seed might perish forever.

We have taken the liberty to allude, in the course of this verse, to the fashion of the times, which is to cram the heads of all those who are ambitious to be stuffed with any quantity of learning. In our allusion we have been a little playful, and for the reason that we see so much in this custom which is ludicrous in the extreme.

One of the most entertaining novels that ever was written could be made up of the over-educated brains, and dry, unsympathetic hearts, of the society of this and other communities of New England. We sincerely trust that some one who has the genius adequate to the work will ere long present us with the ludicrous in the educated circles of New England. Learning has absolutely become an egregious bore, in too many instances. So much is this the case that persons with a fair amount of common sense, and good dispositions, feel themselves to be unsafe among what is termed the "learned world," lest they should discover their ignorance of the ancient and modern languages, the details of history, together with the data of science, the beauties of the poets, the rules of art, and all other matters discussed by the learned ; in the event of which, poor souls, they are liable to the awful fate of being contemptuously classed with the "vulgar." We think there is upon the face of God's green earth no meaner, more despicable object than he or she who makes a parade of their knowledge with a view to embarrass others, — a not infrequent occurrence, in our "highly educated New England society." If some one does not attempt the illustration of these double-refined nosegays — this ludicrous, bombastic scholarship — feeble as we are for the task, we shall, nevertheless, approach it with what power we possess, and knock at least some few feathers from the birds at which we aim.

There is reason in all things; and so, too, there should be reason in the management of one's knowledge. If mere saps of either sex, because they have a certain amount of polite learning in their noddles, are to be encouraged in the assumption and absurdities so glaring in society, it is quite time that the pen of satire, as an avenging sword, should be drawn against them, and wielded with relentless vigor. It is the only means which can save us from running into that sadest of all conditions — literary sottishness.

On reading "Our Modern Athens; or, Who is First?" to a pleasant friend, she looked at us with a fearful countenance, and said, "Do you really mean to publish that? Why, sir, there has been nothing so severe ever given to the public; and though most truthful, it will bring about your ears untold curses."

We replied, that we did not care whom we offended; that we had been impressed to make the attack, and should follow out our purpose. We had been witness to the insolent pride and bearing of the snobs of "Athens," and could not resist the sweet temptation to hiss them heartily. We have not done with them yet, nor shall we desist from our intention of castigating them periodically, until the novelty of our task wears off.

"But, sir," replied our friend, "you have imposed upon yourself a heavy burden. You can never hope to change the ideas which are so offensive to all true refinement, in brains which are incapable of correct notions of life."

"True, true, most true," we interrupted; "we cannot change their ideas, perhaps, but may we not disease them — give them the dysentery or consumption; so that by and by they will disappear."

Our kind friend laughed, and then, with a great deal of gravity, said, "Sir, you are a miracle. Go on, and prosper."

We, too, in our turn, laughed, and wondered how our friend came to speak so much to the point, and so truthfully; for are we not, kind reader, out of the common course of things, to write as we have written of "Our Modern Athens"? If you are a snob you will not, perhaps, deign to answer us; but if you are, on the contrary, a person of virtuous tastes and inclinations, you will unhesitatingly commend our adventure, and do all you can to circulate the document. With such as you we can shake hands honestly. As for all others, *against them we wage an eternal war of laughter and contempt!* Snob! — fare thee well; — remember, the fool has said in his heart there is no God; and the surest way to become a fool is, if you are of the *mass.* gender, to perfume your whiskers; and if of the *fem.* gender, to color your eye-brows, and "cut" the humble.

www.ingramcontent.com/pod-product-compliance
Lightning Source LLC
Chambersburg PA
CBHW020731100426
42735CB00038B/1870